D1590132

TIPS

The First Weeks of
Middle School Chorus

Patrick K. Freer

MONTGOMERY COUNTY PUBLIC SCHOOLS
PROFESSIONAL LIBRARY
850 HUNGERFORD DRIVE
ROCKVILLE, MARYLAND 20850

WITHDRAWN

Published in partnership with
MENC: The National Association for Music Education

ROWMAN & LITTLEFIELD EDUCATION
A division of
ROWMAN & LITTLEFIELD PUBLISHERS, INC.
Lanham • New York • Toronto • Plymouth, UK

MAR 3 0 2011

Published in partnership with MENC: The National Association for Music Education

Published by Rowman & Littlefield Education
A division of Rowman & Littlefield Publishers, Inc.
A wholly owned subsidary of The Rowman & Littlefield Publishing Group, Inc.
4501 Forbes Boulevard, Suite 200, Lanham, Maryland 20706
http://www.rowmaneducation.com

Estover Road, Plymouth PL6 7PY, United Kingdom

Copyright © 2009 by MENC: The National Association for Music Education

All rights reserved. No part of this book may be reproduced in any form or by any electronic or mechanical means, including information storage and retrieval systems, without written permission from the publisher, except by a reviewer who may quote passages in a review.

British Library Cataloguing in Publication Information Available

Library of Congress Cataloging-in-Publication Data

Freer, Patrick K.
  TIPS : the first weeks of middle school chorus / Patrick K. Freer.
    p. cm.
  "Published in partnership with MENC, The National Association for Music Education."
  ISBN 978-1-60709-165-3 (pbk. : alk. paper) — ISBN 978-1-60709-286-5 (electronic)
  1. Choral singing—Instruction and study—Juvenile. 2. School music—Instruction and study. I. MENC, the National Association for Music Education (U.S.) II. Title.
  MT915.F77 2009
  782.5071'2—dc22   2009014428

♾ ™ The paper used in this publication meets the minimum requirements of American National Standard for Information Sciences—Permanence of Paper for Printed Library Materials, ANSI/NISO Z39.48-1992.

Printed in the United States of America

Contents

Chapter One

The Big Six Questions: Who, What, Why, When, Where, and How

As you begin the first weeks of a new school year, it's a safe bet that you have as many questions about your middle school students as they have about you and the experiences they'll have in chorus. There are several questions to thoughtfully consider about the educational and musical opportunities you'll plan for your students. Your answers to the Big Six Questions will help guide you through the first weeks of school.

BIG QUESTION #1:
WHO IS MIDDLE SCHOOL CHORUS FOR?

Related Questions

- What students do I have already?
- What students are not in chorus? Should they be?
- Is there a place for all students in the school choruses?
- Do I unintentionally "turn off" students by having a high-stakes audition process?
- Are there ensembles for all types of changing adolescent voices?
- Do I need to change the prevailing perception in my school about whom chorus is for?

BIG QUESTION #2:
WHAT IS MIDDLE SCHOOL CHORUS FOR?

Related Questions

- Is the purpose to reinforce existing skills or teach new skills to students?
- Where do students learn musical skills if they're not in chorus?
- What do I assume students know? How do I know this is true?
- Is choral repertoire a conduit for teaching?
- Which comes first, high-level learning or high-level performance? Can both exist?
- Do my students want to gain vocal/musical skills for other, non-chorus activities? How do I feel about this? Can I fulfill these student wishes within existing rehearsals?
- Will my contract renewal be conditioned upon my choruses' contest scores? Can I change this?
- Should I speak with my colleagues at the high school to see what my students will experience after they graduate from middle school?
- Should my goal be this year's December concert or should it be a December concert twenty years from now? Will my students be singing in twenty years because of what we do this fall?

BIG QUESTION #3:
WHY IS THERE SUCH A THING
AS MIDDLE SCHOOL CHORUS?

Related Questions

- How does middle school chorus fit into a sequence of choral experiences that begins in elementary school and extends into adulthood?
- Is chorus about music performance or music education, or both?
- Our voices come with us at no monetary expense. Do financial circumstances prevent some students from joining band or orchestra?
- Does chorus provide an opportunity to reach large numbers of students? How many is too many? Too few?
- Should chorus provide a break from academic pressures for students? Does this mean they should only sing easy repertoire? Or is chorus different enough that it's OK to present challenging repertoire?

BIG QUESTION #4:
WHEN DOES MIDDLE SCHOOL CHORUS OCCUR?

Related Questions

- What does my chorus' schedule imply about its role in the academic life of the school?
- If scheduled during the school day, what do I need to know about the students' schedules that will help me understand how chorus fits into the context of their day?
- If scheduled before the school day, how can I encourage students to attend? Do I need to provide food for students who might miss breakfast?
- If scheduled after the school day, how will I deal with scheduling conflicts from sports and other activities? How can I keep students from being caught between competing interests?
- Is my chorus scheduled the way a general music class is scheduled? Does this provide more opportunity for greater depth of instruction?
- Is my chorus scheduled in large blocks of ninety minutes or so? What does this imply for the types of activities and their pacing during that time?
- Is my chorus scheduled in small blocks of twenty minutes or so? What does this imply about warm-ups? Can I teach concepts and skills during the warm-ups to save time?

BIG QUESTION #5:
WHERE DOES MIDDLE SCHOOL CHORUS OCCUR?

Related Questions

- What's more important—the room or the people in it?
- Does it really matter whether chorus meets in a well-equipped music classroom or in a room next to the cafeteria?
- What can I do to make the rehearsal space attractive for students?
- Do I need to purchase equipment and supplies for the room, or can it be made to function adequately for now?
- Do I have to seat students in straight rows or is there flexibility in how the seats are configured?

- If I travel to other teachers' classrooms for chorus, how can I support their teaching by how I enter the room, what I bring along with me, and what I leave behind?
- If I use other teachers' classrooms, what do I need to request of those teachers to make my traveling situation easier? Are my requests reasonable? Are any of my requests trivial (and possibly annoying)?
- Does anyone do something for my situation that goes unnoticed or without thanks?
- Do students have to travel far (or extremely quickly) to get to chorus rehearsal? How should this affect any penalties for late arrival? How should this affect how class begins?
- Does my rehearsal space mimic the performance space? Will I need to acclimate students to a new space as the performance nears?

BIG QUESTION #6:
HOW SHOULD MIDDLE SCHOOL
CHORUS REHEARSALS OCCUR?

Related Questions

- Are my rehearsals specifically planned for young adolescents between the ages of ten and fourteen?
- How should middle school chorus rehearsals be different from elementary, high school, or church choir rehearsals?
- Do I plan for multiple shifts of activity, focus, and grouping within each rehearsal?
- Are my warm-ups related to the repertoire we're doing? Do my warm-ups change daily to reflect my students' needs and the musical content of the rehearsal?
- Do I teach sight-reading and aural skills during each rehearsal? Are these skills segmented from the repertoire or can students apply what they've learned to the repertoire I've chosen?
- Are students encouraged to self-assess their repertoire-related skills and suggest strategies for improvement?

- Are students taught in ways that prepare them for the content and procedures of specific events such as performances and adjudicated festivals?
- Do I run choral rehearsals like the teachers that I've used as models? Is this appropriate? How might this need to change?
- What would my supervisor think if he or she looked inside the doorway of my classroom at any given moment?
- If other students looked inside the doorway to my classroom, would they want to join chorus?

The answers you provide to these questions will give you insight regarding your own philosophy of choral music education. Perhaps the answers will cause you to rethink the relationship between what you feel about choral music education, how it is actually practiced in your classroom, and how it is perceived by your students.

Chapter Two

Setting Up Your Classroom

How does your classroom look to your students? Students like to be in classrooms that are orderly, yet not too formal. They like brightly colored posters and wall art, but not a scene filled with visual clutter. Students like the routine of entering a classroom and proceeding to their familiar spot in the room, but they also like changes to this routine from time to time.

With these things in mind, let's look at some implications for how your classroom might be configured to best meet the needs of your young adolescent singers.

FIRST IMPRESSIONS

- What is immediately visible from the doorway entrance to the room? Does the teacher's desk announce that you are entering "the teacher's space" by visually blocking the room? Or does the entryway open invitingly to "the students' space" with chairs, risers, and other materials ready for their use?
- If possible, consider decorating the doorframe to your room so that students can tell that this is the chorus room as they walk down the hallway. Some schools will allow this, while others will not.
- Has your room been cleaned of clutter? Or are there papers or other items left on the floor by other students? Try to clear these between each class if necessary.
- What visually announces that this is a music room rather than a social studies classroom?

- Will you have music playing on the audio system as students enter the room? Will this music be related to what the students will learn that day?

WALLS

- What is on the classroom walls? What can you alter and what must remain?
- Are preprinted or homemade posters on the walls? Some schools are steering teachers away from commercially produced posters in favor of well-crafted homemade posters and student work.
- Do the images on the walls project the image you want to convey to students and visitors? Do the displayed musical personalities and images relate to the diversity of your students?
- Consider making a bulletin board for each chorus, filling each with information about upcoming concerts, due dates for assignments, the musical accomplishments of students in the chorus, and reminders about vocal health.
- What can be done to reduce visual clutter on the walls without making them barren?
- Are chalkboards and whiteboards erased frequently, or does outdated information dominate the boards?
- Is there a "Wall of Fame" or trophy shelf celebrating previous accomplishments of choruses and singers? If not, now would be a great time to plan for one.

SEATING

- Make certain that chairs are neatly arranged (and rearranged through the day) to convey a sense of order to incoming students.
- If you use risers for seating, is there enough room for students to sit comfortably without bothering one another (intentionally or otherwise!)?
- If fixed seating in chairs or on risers is limited, consider alternatives such as sitting on the floor. You might want to have various sections of your chorus take turns sitting on the floor if space is a problem. Post a regular schedule for this so that students can plan their dress accordingly.

- If students will be sitting on the floor, could carpet squares be purchased or donated?
- Is the seating conducive to optimal physical alignment for singing? Try sitting where students will sit and noticing the effect on your own physical alignment. With this information in mind, what instructions could you give your students to minimize any posture-related concerns?
- If you plan to stand on a podium, notice what this might mean for singers in the front row(s) of your choir. Will they need to lift their chins awkwardly in order to see you?
- There is some research that suggests young adolescents learn best in any situation other than sitting in straight rows. What can you do to break away from "Straight Row Syndrome" at least some of the time?
- Can you arrange your classroom so that fixed seating is located in one area, leaving another area open for group work and movement activities?

OCTAVOS

- Think ahead about how octavos are stored in your classroom. Will you distribute octavos daily to students? Or will students have their own octavos and store them in folders?
- How will you distribute octavos and other materials that are not in preassigned student folders? The distribution of materials can present opportunities for students to disengage from the rehearsal because of a lack of structure. You might wish to:

  o Place octavos near the door for students to pick up as they arrive.
  o Place octavos under each chair.
  o Place the number of octavos needed for each row under the first chair in that row.
  o Assign section leaders and hand those students the octavos for their section as they arrive.

- Conversely, how will students return octavos? You might wish to:

  o Have students return octavos to a prearranged spot near the door as they leave.

o Dismiss the choir by section or row, with students returning octavos as they dismiss.

o Simply reverse the processes by which music was distributed.

- If the school's choral library is stored in your room and is visible to the students, is that storage system visually neat and orderly? Organizing your choral library to make it functional for you is another issue for another time! For now, you can at least make it look well maintained.

INSTRUMENTS AND BOOKS

- Musical instruments can serve as art if you find yourself without the resources to decorate your room. Many percussion instruments are colorful and visually appealing. Think about how these could be stored in your classroom to showcase the color/shape. Placing the instruments on shelves is one solution, especially if there is another shelf above the instruments to block the students from playing the instruments.
- If you have a textbook series in your room, the colorful spines of these books can also serve as splashes of color. Think about how you might take advantage of this within the storage opportunities afforded by your room.
- Where is the piano located? Make sure that it does not block the view of students in the front row of the choir. Ensure that your view is not blocked when you are seated behind the piano. If so, consider purchasing a counter-height barstool to sit on rather than a piano bench.

EQUIPMENT

- Test each piece of equipment in your room to see that it is functioning. Test yourself on each piece of equipment to see that you know how it operates. Report any problems to the appropriate school personnel immediately. Your administrators want you to succeed, and it's likely they'll move quickly to resolve technological issues if you report them as soon as you arrive in the classroom.

- Begin making a wish list of technology for reference when you submit budget requests for the next year.
- If you plan to use technology with your students, notice how many functional pieces of each item you have for use. The number of available headsets, keyboards, audio recorders, or computers may determine how many groups you can form.
- Make certain that all visual images will be visible for each student in the room. If not, where can students locate themselves to better see the images?
- Make certain that audio excerpts will be easily heard in the room. What sounds loud to you at the front of the room may not be easily audible in other locations around the room.
- If you have any concerns about the safety of the technology in your room, be sure to request locking systems from your administrators. School personnel will need to retain keys for these systems, so it's best not to purchase them without prior approval.
- Make certain to request that all pianos in the building (your classroom, rehearsal areas, stage) are serviced and tuned by a piano technician prior to the first day of school.
- If there are more than two or three music stands in your room, think through how these will be stored when not in use—perhaps a designated storage area or rack system.
- Check to see that all music stands are tightened, greased, and functional.
- Make sure you have thought through safety issues for any personal equipment you may bring to class.

YOUR OWN SPACE

- Create a space—perhaps a corner—that is your space. This space should be only yours, and not for student use. Think about how you can minimize student access to this space by configuring it to thwart student curiosity.
- Make certain this space conveys your personality. Some schools encourage the posting of personal effects such as carefully selected family photographs, diplomas, or other materials related to music and teaching.

You may wish to create duplicates of these materials for posting in your classroom.

- Above all, your classroom needs to be comfortable for both you and your students. Consider bringing in area rugs, lamps, and other meaningful, cozy elements. You'll spend lots of time in this space so try and make it somewhere you'll want to be.

Chapter Three

Meeting and Greeting Your Students

Just as the way you set up your room gives students ideas about what to expect in chorus, the first interactions you have with students let them know that they'll grow to trust you as a teacher and like you as a person.

The first day should not be about rules and regulations, especially for choruses of students you don't know or students for whom chorus is a required class. If your school mandates that you discuss such issues on the first day, do what you can to dispense the information as quickly as possible so that you can get directly to making music. See chapter 4, "Choral Activities on the First Day and Beyond," for some ideas. Middle school students are very receptive to new ideas on the first day of school, despite possible outward appearances of disinterest. If you can get kids singing comfortably and with enjoyment on the first day—"Chorus = Singing"—then you've laid a solid foundation for choral work in succeeding rehearsals. If, instead, students leave your classroom on Day One with the impression that "Chorus = Rules," it will be extremely difficult to coax reluctant singers to become engaged afterward. Do whatever you can to prevent students from thinking, "I love music, but I don't like school music." This should be your mission for the first weeks of school!

Here are some things to think about as you contemplate greeting your students on the first day:

- Stand by the door and greet students as they enter. Place a sign just inside the door directing students where to sit so that you can remain in the doorway.
- Stay in the doorway for a few minutes beyond the official starting time of class to greet students who are unfamiliar with the school/schedule

and are running late. Their anxiety level will be heightened, and your calm welcome will be a relief to them.

- If many students are late to class on the first day, begin by asking why and what you can do to help them be on time. The first day is not the time to chastise students for being tardy; it's the time for modeling good problem-solving skills and letting students see that you'll listen to their points of view.
- If possible, greet students by name. If you don't know the students, ask them their names when they arrive at the door and repeat the names as you greet them.
- Consider shaking hands with the students as they enter. Many youngsters never learn how to shake hands properly, and this can be an opportunity to reinforce a social skill while making a good first impression.
- Give students index cards and have them obtain a pen or pencil. Have them write on the index card, listing their names and whatever personal information you wish to have, such as phone numbers (both student and parent), e-mail addresses, and previous musical experiences.

  o On the index card, have students complete the sentence, "If I could learn anything in chorus, I'd like to learn . . ."
  o Compile this information and use it during succeeding rehearsals, either to directly inform lesson content or to use as motivators throughout the year ("I saw that many of you want to sing lead in your band. One difference between singing into a microphone and singing in a chorus is . . .").

- When establishing behavior parameters during the first weeks of school, do what you can to promote the behavior you wish to see. If you want students to take their seats quickly, consider placing a musical problem on the board as students enter (a sight-reading example, perhaps). Make solving this puzzle into a challenge where, for instance, the first section to sing it accurately receives a bonus grade. Tardy students will not receive the bonus grade, even if their section wins the challenge for that day.

  o If you have multiple choirs meeting at different times, consider using the same musical problem for all choirs and record the results on the board. The challenge will then extend between the choirs.

o It's easy to begin class with sight-reading activities construed as challenges. This gets the students focused on lesson content from the first moments. Remember, only tradition states that choral rehearsals have to begin with warm-ups!

o Also, these types of activities minimize the embarrassment of students who arrive late. They allow you to deal with individual student issues while the larger group is focused elsewhere. They allow you to get a sense of the group dynamic before launching into the formal part of your rehearsal.

- If you wish to use "quiet signals" in your classroom, let students know what the quiet signal will be. This sounds obvious, but you'd be surprised at how many teachers give quiet signals that are completely ignored by students.
- Think about how you want to address students.

o At the middle school level, "men and women" seems as out of place as "boys and girls." The students aren't really "sopranos, altos, tenors, and baritones" either. Look for other terminologies that work well for you.

o One very successful middle school choral teacher uses the term "sports fans," as in, "Hey, all you sports fans, turn to page 6." This teacher uses sports memorabilia to decorate her room, with items ranging from the National Football League to figure skating and everything in between. She then captions each item with a homemade sign, such as "Look at the [u] vowel on this guy's lips!" to reinforce vocal/choral concepts. These offer moments to show interest beyond school choral music, draw students into conversations about athletics, allow for the teacher to make analogies between sports and choral music, and inject a healthy dose of humor into the classroom environment.

More than anything, let your students know that you care about them, their musicianship, and their contribution to the chorus. Your students' impressions of you begin on the first day. Give some thought to how those impressions are formed so that you make the first day as successful for you as it is for your students!

Chapter Four

Choral Activities on
the First Day and Beyond

The following activities can be done with any choir at any time. However, they work especially well on the first day of class when students are the most eager to please. Singing and making music in a nonthreatening way on the first day of school encourages students to feel positive about the experience and eager to return to the following rehearsal.

What do you do when the students don't know any repertoire? Try these ideas:

ECHO CHAINS

Begin by dividing the class into at least four rows, then sing a one-measure unit of solfège to the first row (G to E range—the composite unison range of middle school choirs). The first row turns and sings it to the next row, and immediately turns back for a new, overlapping measure of solfège. To end, simply stop supplying new melodies, and the echo will eventually end with the back row. *Variation:* incorporate both repetition (literal echo) and variation (improvised response).

MODAL MANIA

Begin by choosing a key. The major scale (starting on *do*) of that key is the Ionian mode, and the minor scale (starting on *la*) of that key is the Aeolian mode, and so forth. Divide the class into groups and have each group sing a modal scale (up then down or visa versa) so that pairs or

17

trios of modes sound simultaneously. A pair of modes that works well to begin is Phrygian and Ionian, and then Mixolydian can be added as a third mode. Take care when choosing modes for each group so that students are able to sing the mode that is selected for them. If your choir has singers who cannot sing an octave beginning on any pitch, then limit the scale to the range of a fifth. As a reminder, these are the typical modes in the key of C:

C-C	Ionian
B-B	Locrian
A-A	Aeolian
G-G	Mixolydian
F-F	Lydian
E-E	Phrygian
D-D	Dorian
C-C	Ionian

ALEATORIC AMALGAMATION

Begin by teaching all students a familiar song with a range no more than a sixth (such as "Friendship Song"; Boosey & Hawkes, M051466160; changing the key to fit the needs of the changing voices). Then number students 1–5 (or more if desired), where students sing the melody but instead of the printed rhythm, they sing each pitch for the number of beats corresponding to their assigned number. Sing through twice on words or syllables and conclude by sustaining a hummed *do*. The overlapping pitches and unexpected harmonies make this a favorite with both students and, when performed during a concert, with audiences.

JAZZ CIRCLES

Introduce the activity by singing a melodic ostinato pattern within the G to E range. Ask students to suggest variations that they could perform, perhaps assisting them by providing specific scat syllables or rhythm patterns. Ask for and then practice several more variations. Choose a small group of students to maintain the ostinato pattern while others experiment with variations. Have students determine how to begin and end the piece.

Next, divide the class into several groups that will work together in different locations around the room for approximately five minutes. Each group will have the tasks of:

- creating a vocal improvisation around the specified ostinato,
- maintaining the ostinato part with at least one group member,
- involving all group members in a vocal, improvised performance, and
- planning and performing a beginning and an ending.

Have the groups perform for each other and follow with focused questions: "Which group changed the key?" "Which groups had a coda?" "Which group used ABA form?" and so forth.

By varying your instructions to the students, this activity can be either simple or complex. I've had success using twelve-bar blues form, but the range of the ostinato (the traditional bass line) is often not possible for young adolescents. In that case, I've often played the twelve-bar blues chords (key of B minor) on the piano while students improvise around my accompaniment. I've even used this as a piece on a concert program. I've explained the process to the audience, they've watched the students perform the improvisation, and then I've asked the audience to join in!

SPEECHIFYING SPECTACLE

This activity gives students some structured vocal exploration where the use of pitch is not required. Start by providing a line of text. Perhaps this can be from your repertoire, that day's newspaper, or a student-authored poem. Read the text in several ways, such as only speaking the voiced consonants, only speaking the vowels, or only speaking every other word. Experiment by choosing one or two lines, elongating the vowels or consonants, varying dynamics, and playing with various tempi. Record the examples and play back for discussion and analysis. An extension would be to divide students into groups, each presenting their "speechifying spectacle" to the rest of the choir, and having the choir members guess which text was used.

SOUND BALL

Toss a soft, light ball (underhand) to a student and sing/speak a nonsense syllable. Ask the student to catch the ball and repeat the sound to you, then toss it back using a new sound. Hint: have students identify to whom they will toss the ball before the game begins.

Variation 1: Gather students into a circle to play sound ball. Add two rules: (1) always make your partner look good, no matter if they drop the ball or not; and (2) always say "yes" by making eye contact before tossing the ball.

Variation 2: Play sound ball, except use favorite food names. Figure out how many syllables are in the food names students will use, and momentarily practice singing each syllable on a different pitch of the student's choice. Proceed to play sound ball with the food names. (No need to repeat the food of the pitcher in this version.)

Variation 3: Use three balls of different sizes and colors. Using only those pitches that are common to all students in the group, select pitches to be *do* (largest ball), *mi* (medium ball), and *sol* (small ball). Students pass the balls either by tossing across the circle or by passing to the person next to them. Students sing the pitch/syllable corresponding to the ball they receive and sustain that pitch (staggering the breath) until they receive another ball and switch to that pitch/syllable.

Variation 4: Have students choose any phrase of a song (perhaps from their current choral repertoire) and sing it when the ball is tossed to them. You might use this as a game to assist with memorizing a song, asking that phrases be sung in order from the beginning of the song to the end, but students have to sing their appropriate voice part . . . quite a challenge!

"WHOOSH, WHOA"

This is a great game for a nonstressful vocalization activity. The variations are limitless, and specific directions can change the game into almost anything that relates to the goal of your particular lesson. This is especially good for focusing attention, getting students to laugh and interact, and for incorporating physical motion with the onset of phonation.

Place students in a circle. Explain that the syllable "whoosh" is going to be sung with a high pitch of the students' choosing and has a corresponding motion of tipping a basketball into the hoop with both arms overhead; this combination of sound and motion passes the "whoosh" to the next person in the circle.

Practice passing the "whoosh" with a sustained "ooh" vowel and the overhead hand motion. Next, add the syllable "whoa" and its corresponding motion of passing a bowling ball (both hands underhand) to the next person in the circle. Practice passing the "whoa" on a low pitch with a sustained "ooh" vowel and the underhand motion. Next, send both the "whoosh" and the "whoa" around the circle simultaneously, but in opposite directions (the "whoosh" and "whoa" will cross at some point, utterly confusing the lucky player!).

Variation 1: If the circle is especially large, insert other motions/ syllables into the mix to keep more students involved at one time. Adding body percussion is especially effective, either as single sounds or as part of short rhythmic phrases.

Variation 2: Again, if the group is especially large, divide the class into two groups, one smaller than the other. The smaller group forms an inner circle within the larger circle of students. The groups then perform "whoosh, whoa" the same way, or the two groups could do different activities, such as "sound ball" (above).

Chapter Five

Repertoire for Any Choir's First Weeks

The eleven pieces listed here will work with almost any choir of any age. That doesn't mean that you won't need some creativity, however! Three key principles apply: know your singers, know your learners, and know your repertoire.

KNOW YOUR SINGERS

- Before choosing any piece of music, know what to expect from the vocal capabilities of your students. If don't know your students, there are a few reliable vocal characteristics of young adolescents:
  - o Girls are basically young sopranos, and they can sing much higher pitches than typically found in middle school repertoire.
  - o Boys will have many different ranges, especially in seventh and eighth grade choruses.

- The composite unison range of any mixed group of middle school singers is approximately a sixth, from G to E in octaves. This *is probably not* the range for any individual student in your choir—it is the range that all students will have *in common*. Most students will be able to sing higher and/or lower than this limited unison range.

KNOW YOUR LEARNERS

- It is easier for novice middle school students to sing melodies with step-wise motion than melodies with many awkward intervals.
- It is easier for novice middle school students to sing ascending intervals than descending intervals.
- Most novice middle school students find it harder to sing in foreign languages than in English because they may follow the printed words rather than the musical notation. You can work on this later—get them singing first! Rote teaching can be effective in this situation.
- When presenting musical notation, be certain that your boys know how to read bass clef. If not, an A below middle C (top line, bass clef) will look to be an F one and one-half octaves above middle C (top line, treble clef). Many middle school boys will respond with "it's too high" when they just need help reading the correct clef!
- If basic notation or navigating a choral score is new and/or difficult, could beginning repertoire be taught by rote? Through word sheets? With an overhead or LCD projector? Again, first things first.
- What do your students need to experience success from the very first encounter with choral music?

KNOW YOUR REPERTOIRE

- Know your pitches, rhythms, pronunciations, and "road-map" for the repertoire. No excuses.
- Know how to play any accompaniments or vocal lines on the piano if necessary.
- For the first days of school, choose repertoire that everyone can sing. If you don't know your students, choose repertoire limited to the G-E composite unison range discussed above.
- Analyze your favorite, easy rounds and repertoire. If any of these have vocal lines encompassing a sixth, transpose them into the correct key for your choir—possibly to the keys of G, A flat, or A to allow for unison singing between G and E.

ELEVEN PIECES TO START THE SCHOOL YEAR

These eleven pieces have been chosen because they are from the standard choral repertory, have stood the test of time, and incorporate a limited vocal range. Many of these pieces appear on various state festival and contest lists. Each piece works very well for initial choral experiences, and several might be programmed together to form an effective concert in October—which some schools expect!

1. "The Black Snake Wind" (arr. Mary Goetze)
   SSA with piano
   Boosey & Hawkes, #M051461233
   Notes: This is a classic introduction to part-singing. Melodies begin on a unison pitch and then diverge—mostly descending. The piece is in ABA form and minimalist in style and duration (only three pages in length). The B section begins with a unison canonic entrance for all parts. The key will need to be changed, probably to the key of G minor, and sung in octaves for changing boys' voices. Consider adding a flute or recorder to the melody line of the interlude.
2. "Come Sail Away with Me"
   Order using the title "Two Unison Songs for Male Chorus" (by Mark Patterson)
   Unison with piano (though some sources list it as TB voicing)
   BriLee Music, #BL472
   Notes: Despite the "male chorus" designation, this piece works equally well for mixed choirs in octaves. The piece is a brief lullaby (or love song) that feels substantial, is in ABA form, and has some appealing syncopation. This is a fine example of how to write singable melodies with only five or six pitches. The second piece in the collection, "The British Grenadiers," is also fine, though not for the first days of school.
3. "Come Today with Jubilant Singing" (by Robert Leaf)
   Unison with piano
   GIA, #G-2325
   Notes: This piece presents a wealth of teaching opportunities. The ABA structure provides contrasts of melodic contour, expression, and dynamics. A return to the opening "A" material demonstrates augmentation and

diminution (you don't have to reteach the pitches!). You may wish to alter the pitches at the ends of two phrases ending on a low E if they are too low for boys singing an octave lower than printed.

4. "Da Pacem Domine" (by Melchior Franck, arr. Mary Goetze)
Four-part treble
Boosey & Hawkes, #M051461875
Notes: This canon can be sung in any combination between two and four parts. The second voice of the canon is imitative, not literal. It is generally not necessary to change the printed key if sung in octaves. As printed, the four parts conclude in a harmonically rich cadence. It is possible to sing without this ending, though it provides a clear introduction to navigating a choral score (especially if you use colored ink to highlight student parts).

5. "Feel Good" (arr. Barbara Baker and David Elliott)
Three-part treble
Boosey & Hawkes, #M051467112
Notes: The form of the piece is AB-bridge-AB. The "A" melody is unison, and the first four measures can be sung at pitch by most middle school boys, dropping to an octave lower on the first note of the fifth measure. The "B" section is three-part homophony, with each part encompassing a different limited range. Work within the existing key to identify the best part for the students in your choir, singing in octaves as needed.

6. "Five Rounds for Changing Voices" (by Elliot Levine)
Unison
Shadow Press, #SP206
Notes: These rounds were designed for beginning middle school choirs and the texts are appealingly adolescent. Though most encompass more than the interval of a sixth, several basically combine mini-canons within the larger canon. Find opportunities where boys with limited tessituras can sing one of these mini-canons and have them sing that part through the entire piece rather than singing the other mini-canons that may not suit their voices. As always, change keys as needed.

7. "Friendship Song" (Czech canon, arr. Doreen Rao)
Unison
Boosey & Hawkes, #M051466160
Notes: This canon has the range of a sixth and the canon can begin in any measure. The descending line is ideal for novice singers. Sing in the key of G or A. The English text is printed, but it can be problem-

atic—many "eh" vowels can lead to the spreading of vowels. Try singing on solfège, "loo" numbers, or even sing in Czech.

8. "Kabo Kabo"

Order using the title "Three Yoruba Native Songs of Nigeria" (arr. Henry Leck)

Unison with percussion

Colla Voce, #21-20514

Notes: This is the third in the collection of three songs. The range is a fifth, but the key will need to be changed upward, possibly as much as a fourth. The text is challenging to pronounce, but only because of the tempo. Rhythms are repetitive and energetic. The piece is drawn from a welcome song for a king—a good initial piece for a concert program. The other two pieces in the collection have wider ranges but are equally viable for middle school choruses.

9. "Niska Banja" (arr. Nick Page)

SAAB with piano

Boosey & Hawkes, #M051465170

Notes: The infectious rhythm should be taught as the introductory experience, using body percussion to establish the pattern. The piece contains only ten measures of melodic material. A clear pronunciation guide is provided. The piece is structured so that soloists or a small group could sing the middle section. A strong pianist is required, with 1-piano/4-hands notated in the score. Three of the four parts are limited in range to a sixth or less (one sings a single pitch for eight measures!), but the piano part requires that the piece be performed in the printed key. Assign the parts, in octaves, to match the limited ranges of your students.

10. "Somagwaza" (arr. Pete Seeger)

SATB

World Music Press, #07

Notes: The SATB designation is misleading; the piece is essentially three layered ostinati, with each ostinato sung by a different group of singers. Disregard the voice part designations in the printed score (your sopranos may even get to read from the bass clef!). The ranges of the ostinati are different, so match the printed ostinati with the ranges of your singers. Changing the key slightly upward is usually required for middle school choruses. Recordings of this piece are available through MP3 download sites, including a few sung by massive crowds of people at Pete Seeger concerts.

11. "Yonder Come Day" (Georgia Sea Isles, arr. Judith Cook Tucker)
    Three-part
    World Music Press, #10
    Notes: This piece is a three-part partner song. Each part has a different limited range. Singing in octaves, match the limited ranges of your singers to the limited ranges of the printed vocal lines. This can be performed as printed with nearly any choir, but feel free to change the key if desired. A speech chorus is included with the third vocal line performing an ostinato accompaniment (perfect for boys with changing voices).

Chapter Six

Basics of Warm-ups
for Changing Voices

The following are some key points about warming up middle school choirs. It is important to remember that warm-ups are singing, and the unison singing that won't work for repertoire won't work for warm-ups. The composite unison range of any middle school choir is approximately a sixth, from G to E in octaves. So even if you start on a note that every student can sing, any *do-mi-sol* vocalise will have left some students behind after the third ascending repetition.

As with most middle school experiences, we need to invite students to join rather than demand that they sing for us. Especially for those in the midst of voice change or those who are reluctant to sing, it is important that we begin warm-ups with pitches and activities that suit their needs. The following suggestions are intended to prompt your thinking about ways to meet the needs of all your adolescent singers during your warm-up procedures and beyond.

A warm-up is:

• a sequence of activities focused on the coordination of vocal skills in preparation for the challenges of a specific rehearsal.

KEY COMPONENTS OF A SUCCESSFUL WARM-UP
SESSION FOR YOUNG ADOLESCENTS ARE:

• a logical sequence that remains consistent from day to day.
• an allowance for student choice and experimentation within the procedures.

- a clear pedagogical relationship between the tasks of the warm-up session and the repertoire to follow.
- an allowance for a variety of student groupings, bodily movements, and physical locations within the warm-up session.

The five stages of the sequential warm-up session are:

- Relaxation: Draw imagery from everyday life, like weather, getting ready for school, sports, and so on.
- Alignment/Posture: Focus on optimal alignment of each individual body rather than rules and restrictions (one size doesn't fit all!).
- Breathing: Remember exhalation before inhalation.
- Phonation/Resonance

  o Begin as pitch nonspecific, move toward pitch-specific.
  o Onset of sound occurs on the breath inflow and just continues as pitches flow through.
  o Connect breathflow to soundflow—for instance, humming and chewing.
  o Always descend first on [u]; also descend first for vocalises, by half-steps from a comfortable middle pitch—contrary to traditional practice!
  o The goal is a "melted transition" between light and heavy mechanisms ("registers").

- Vocalization and Sung Exercises

  o Vocalise: a complete, miniature musical composition (implied V-I cadence).
  o Sequence of vocalises for voice conditioning:

    ▪ gradually higher and higher pitches
    ▪ gradually louder and louder volumes
    ▪ faster and faster speeds of laryngeal/vocal tract muscular movement
    ▪ finally, the lowest four or five producible pitches

  o Draw from the pedagogical needs of the students and the repertoire. Make the application apparent to students.
  o Consider ending the final vocalise in the key of the piece to follow.

o Consider placing vocalises throughout the rehearsal when they're most effective at preparing for challenges—not just the beginning!

Remember—the warm-up sequence is a great opportunity for you to teach skills and present solutions to problems you anticipate later in the rehearsal. Identifying and analyzing these necessary skills only comes from studying your scores and having a plan for the rehearsal. Waiting until the students sing to decide what to do is too late. Use the warm-ups to prepare for the rehearsal to follow.

Used effectively, the warm-up sequence provides the best possible teaching tool for choral music teachers.

NOTE

Background material for this chapter is drawn from the book *Bodymind and Voice*, edited by Leon Thurman and Graham Welch (The VoiceCare Network et al., 2000).

Chapter Seven

Rehearsal Strategies

Middle school students need changes of activity, focus, or location about every twelve minutes or so. More than just moving to another piece in the repertoire, this means that we have to be creative about teaching strategies within the choral rehearsal. The techniques described below are just a starting point for your imagination. These ideas, coupled with your own student-centered innovations, will keep your students enthused while reinforcing the musical concepts of the rehearsal.

REHEARSAL DESIGN AND PACING

Timekeeper

Give a specific amount of time to rehearsal segments. Let a student tell you when time is up; if time expires, you need to ask permission to borrow more time. This works especially well with a student who has attentional difficulties!

Opposing Teams

Divide class into two or three groups (by voice part or ensembles); students sing only when conducted by you. Alternate groups by phrases, pages, and so on. For extra challenge, assign a blank wall as a group— silence will ensue when you conduct the wall for a phrase (this forces students to audiate).

ASSESSMENT OF STUDENT NEEDS FOR LEARNING

Detail Detector

Let students examine the score of a new piece for any markings or notation that they do not understand; this will give an indication of what concepts and skills need to be taught before the piece itself.

Range Inspector

Assuming that students are aware of their current ranges and tessituras (for example, via the Developing Voice Bulletin Board described in *Getting Started with Middle School Chorus, Second Edition*), students can examine potential pieces for singability; this allows students to have substantive input regarding repertoire used in class. You can certainly limit the choices to ensure that specific styles or genres are included in the repertory.

SUPPORTING AND ASSESSING STUDENT LEARNING

Jump Start

When students are in groups, each group can ask for a specified number of "jump starts." These will be moments of teacher assistance that you will provide in response to specific needs identified by the students.

Dynamic Feet

Have students stamp (lightly!) their feet to the rhythm of their vocal line while remaining vocally silent. The stamping should reflect the dynamics of the printed vocal line, including crescendos, decrescendos, and so on. This works especially well with polyphonic music. The accompaniment might be played if applicable.

INCORPORATING GROUP WORK AND COLLABORATION

Singing Circles

Depending on the situation, circles can be small or large, homogeneous or heterogeneous. Each voice part may form an individual circle, or you might have multiple concentric circles.

LEARNER-CENTERED REHEARSAL TECHNIQUES

Target Practice

Use a dart board and a brightly-colored dart (point removed) to visually gauge how close students came to the "bull's-eye" of meeting a challenge within the choral rehearsal. Follow with specific feedback about what was accomplished and what will follow.

Music Minus Me

Number off the choir by the number of pages in a piece of music; each student does not sing on their corresponding numbered page, but instead listens to the choir around him or her and provides specific feedback at the conclusion of the rehearsal segment.

Memory Pictures

When memorizing a piece, have students utilize their varying learning style preferences by, for instance, drawing pictures that represent the text. Display these at the front of the room and use as sign-posts when beginning to sing from memory. This can also work with dance/movement gestures.

Think-Pair-Share

This is the classic cooperative learning strategy of having pairs of singers turn to each other quickly to discuss a problem and/or pose a solution. This works well when having students experiment with multiple ways of doing something (like tongue position on an [i], and so forth).

Musical Prediction

Before handing out a new piece of music, read the text aloud. Predict how the composer would have set each musical element (melody, harmony, rhythm, timbre, texture, form, dynamics) based on the text only. Compare the predictions with the printed score.

Sound Off

Distribute a new piece of music. From the printed score alone (no sound), ask students how the composer set each musical element and how they arrived at their answers. This facilitates the navigating of choral scores when you use a system for identifying locations within the music, such as by page-system-measure ("2-3-5" equals page 2, system 3, measure 5).

Substitute Plans

Imagine (if necessary) that you will not be present for the next day's rehearsal. Ask students to write the lesson plan that the substitute teacher will need to follow. Be as specific about methods, techniques, and time limits as practical. When you arrive the next day, teach the lesson exactly as the students indicated. If you wish, you might pretend to be a different person (the substitute), complete with different dress and mannerisms—much to your students' amusement! Discuss afterward about how to improve on the lesson plan next time.

Chapter Eight

Placing Students into Groups and Voice Parts

How do you arrange your students into groups and voice parts when you hardly know them? While it's important that groups be assigned so that repertoire work can begin, it's also important that the process be efficient and orderly. Once everyone begins singing, the following procedure should take no more than fifteen minutes, even for large choruses. OK—maybe the first time will take a bit longer, but the procedure will move very quickly once you have some practice. These ideas have been adapted from the work of John Cooksey and Lynne Gackle, and some of the procedures reflect their research about adolescent changing voices. For the purposes of this chapter, the specific voice classifications of Cooksey and Gackle have been replaced with more general terms. You can find more detailed information in *Getting Started with Middle School Chorus, Second Edition*.

STEP 1

Prepare by placing a grand staff on a chalkboard, whiteboard, or a bulletin board. The bulletin board option is preferred so that you can keep it on display for the entire year. Fill the grand staff with measures, and then draw the range of each voice part you will be using as a basis for your groups. The voice parts used in the following procedure are the following:

Girls: Treble A (lighter voices; all adolescent girls have young soprano ranges)
          Treble B (darker voices; all adolescent girls have young soprano ranges)

Boys: Part I (unchanged voices)
          Part II (lower treble voices)
          Part III (early changing voice, lowest note A below middle C)
          Part IV (middle changing voice, lowest note F below middle C)
          Part V (lower changing voice, lowest note D below middle C)
          Part VI (young baritone voice)

STEP 2

Give students 3 x 5 colored index cards from which they cut out a quarter note. Have students write their name on their quarter note.

STEP 3

Divide class into two groups by gender. Groups stand around the piano, or wherever is most convenient given your room configuration.

STEP 4

Have everyone sing "Jingle Bells" (range of a fifth) in the key of C (first note: E).

- Those who sing in the treble clef range: Treble A and B, Parts I, II, and III
- Those who choose the bass clef range: Parts V and VI
- Those who struggle to be comfortable: Part IV

STEP 5

Ask boys to sing "Jingle Bells" as a group in the key of C (first note: E). Listen for those singing in the bass clef range; tap these boys on the shoulder. Ask just these boys to sing "Jingle Bells" again in the key of C. *Do not specify the octave in which they are to sing.*

- Those who sing the higher notes (*mi* to *sol*) but struggle with *do*: Part IV
- Those who sing in the treble clef range: Parts I, II, and III
- Any boys who instinctively choose falsetto: Parts IV, V, and VI
- Those who sing easily in the bass clef range: Parts V and VI (as before)
- For those who do not match pitch, listen carefully to the notes they do sing:

  o Below the pitch: Parts V and VI
  o Above the pitch: Parts II, III, and IV

STEP 6

Seat the "baritones" in their own area of the choir: Parts V and VI.

STEP 7

Ask remaining boys to sing "Jingle Bells" in the key of F (first note A). Listen for those singing in the upper octave with ease; tap these boys on the shoulder; they are Parts I or II.

- Seat Part I boys (those with "lighter" voices) next to or with Treble A girls.
- Seat Part II boys (those with "darker" or "more mature" voices) next to Treble B girls; they can sing an alto part or a tenor part that does not go lower than the G below middle C (the lowest part in a typical three-part mixed selection).
- Once seated, have the Part II boys stand and sing again in the key of F. Any who are singing in falsetto should remove themselves from the group—falsetto indicates a further stage of voice change.

STEP 8

The remaining boys should be Parts III and IV. Ask them to sing "Jingle Bells" in the key of G♭ (first note: B♭ below middle C). They can sing a tenor part that does not go lower than E below middle C (a typical SATB tenor part). Seat Parts III and IV next to the Part II boys.

STEP 9

Have girls stand and sing "Jingle Bells" in the key of C (first note: E). Notice the girls who are singing most comfortably with the most clear voices; touch these girls on the shoulder. These girls may tentatively be assigned to the Treble B part.

STEP 10

Have all girls sing "Jingle Bells" in the key of G (first note: B). Notice girls who are singing most comfortably; touch these girls on the shoulder.

- These girls may tentatively be assigned to the Treble A part.
- Girls who were tapped both times can be evenly divided between the two treble parts; reassess the accuracy of these placements at a later time.
- Girls who were not tapped may be evenly divided between the two treble parts. Reassess the accuracy of these placements at a later time.

FOR ALL-BOYS CHOIRS

When using a group classification procedure in an all-boys group, simply divide into three groups:

- High (Parts I and II)
- Middle (Parts III and IV)
- Low (Parts V and VI)

Will this be perfect? Absolutely not! But, it will be close. The beauty of the process is that you can require students to sing in the group to which they have been assigned. However, any student who feels he or she has been placed incorrectly can arrange to see you for a private voice placement hearing. This is a great way to accomplish a huge task in a minimum amount of time while encouraging students to become aware of their personal vocal development.

Suggested Resources
for the First Weeks of School

Carter, T. (2005). *Choral charisma: Singing with expression*. Santa Barbara, CA: Santa Barbara Music Publishing.

Freer, P. K. (2005). *Success for adolescent singers: Unlocking the potential in middle school choirs* [DVD video series]. Waitsfield, VT: Choral Excellence. (www.choralexcellence.com)

Freer, P. K. (2009). *Getting started with middle school chorus* (2nd ed.). Lanham, MD: MENC/Rowman & Littlefield Education.

Herrington, J., & Miller, C. (2000). *Lame brain games*. San Pedro, CA: Pavane Publishing.

McGill, S., & Volk, E. (2008). *Beyond singing: Blueprint for the exceptional choral program*. Milwaukee, WI: Hal Leonard.

Neuen, D. (2003). *Empower the choir! Concepts for singers*. Waitsfield, VT: Choral Excellence, Inc. (www.choralexcellence.com)

Robinson, R. L. (2006). *Creative rehearsal techniques for today's choral classroom* [DVD]. Van Nuys, CA: Alfred Publishing.

Willetts, S. (2000). *Beyond the downbeat: Choral rehearsal skills and techniques*. Nashville, TN: Abingdon Press.

About the Author

Patrick K. Freer is associate professor of choral music education at Georgia State University in Atlanta. He has been the director of choral activities at Salisbury University (MD), the education director of Young Audiences of New Jersey, and, for eleven years, taught public school music at all grade levels. Dr. Freer holds B.M. and M.M. degrees from Westminster Choir College of Rider University and an Ed.D. from Teachers College, Columbia University. He is the author of numerous resources for choral music teachers, including the critically acclaimed DVD series *Success for Adolescent Singers: Unlocking the Potential in Middle School Choirs*.

Dr. Freer is a frequent guest conductor for all-state and regional honors choruses. He has presented at numerous national and international conferences, including the national meetings of MENC and ACDA, with additional presentations in thirty-one states. Some of Dr. Freer's articles have appeared in *Music Educators Journal, Choral Journal, Music Education Research, Research Studies in Music Education, Philosophy of Music Education Review*, and the *Journal of Music Teacher Education*. Dr. Freer has served on Editorial Boards for the *International Journal of Music Education, Music Educators Journal*, and the *Middle Grades Research Journal*.

Breinigsville, PA USA
11 August 2010
243389BV00002B/2/P